Babylon

CITY OF WONDERS

Babylon

CITY OF WONDERS

Irving Finkel & Michael Seymour

THE BRITISH MUSEUM PRESS

BABYLON: MYTH AND REALITY
Exhibition organised by the British Museum, the Musée du Louvre
and the Réunion des Musées Nationaux, Paris and the Staatliche
Museen zu Berlin.

   S M
B Staatliche Museen
zu Berlin

Irving Finkel and Michael Seymour have asserted the right to be
identified as the authors of this work.

First published in 2008 by
The British Museum Press
A division of The British Museum Company Ltd
38 Russell Square, London WC1B 3QQ
www.britishmuseum.org

A catalogue record for this book is available from the British Library

ISBN   978 0 7141 1171 1

Designed and typeset by Turchini Design
Printed by Graphicom SrL in Italy

FRONTISPIECE
Panel from Nebuchadnezzar's throne-room at Babylon, reconstructed
in the Staatliche Museen zu Berlin, Vorderasiatisches Museum.

The papers used in this book are natural, recyclable products and the
manufacturing processes conform to the environmental regulations of the
country of origin.

CONTENTS

Babylon, Gate of the Gods
The Ishtar Gate, the most spectacular feature of Nebuchadnezzar's
new Babylon, restored to its former glory in the Vorderasiatisches
Museum, Berlin. The name of the city literally means 'Gate of the Gods'.

PREFACE

Ancient Babylon was truly a city of wonders. It holds a unique place in the world: one of the great capitals of Antiquity, the fulfilment of unbounded architectural dreams, and the centre of a great empire. At the same time, Babylon proved to be a gateway through which passed some of the greatest names of history, as well as the lasting ideas of story-tellers, mathematicians and thinkers.

The city, its life and achievements, and the fate of its most famous dynasty are absorbing enough, but the wider role that developed from historical events at Babylon gave a further life to the city and its reputation, just as the place itself, after many complexities and dramas, began to decline in reality. Nebuchadnezzar's Babylon, so beleaguered by the Old Testament Prophets as a City of Sin, became a lasting symbol ever after. Painters, artists, writers and musicians have been in thrall to the Tower of Babel, the fabled Gardens, and the interplay of sin and punishment, reputation and morality.

In this book we have attempted to reflect something of the richness and wonder of the real Babylon, from which so many later myths and legends sprang.

INTRODUCTION

The ancient city

Babylon lies in southern Iraq on the river Euphrates, about eighty-five kilometres south of Baghdad.

The city's political status was first established by King Hammurapi (known today for his Code of Laws) in the eighteenth century BC, but Babylon achieved its greatest glory during the long and stable reign of King Nebuchadnezzar II (605–562 BC). During this time Babylon was the largest and most important city in the world.

The remains which are visible today at the site give little idea of the architectural magnificence of which its ancient kings were so proud. For Babylon, a sprawling, cosmopolitan metropolis at the centre of a great empire, was home to the most lavish palaces and temples, built to accommodate the needs of human and divine authority. The ziggurat, or stepped temple-tower, dominated the skyline of the city, while great encircling walls protected the bustling capital. Built of clay bricks intended to last for eternity, these structures eventually succumbed to decay and dismantling, until ultimately they were lost from sight altogether.

For three thousand years the peoples of ancient Iraq wrote in cuneiform script on tablets of clay. Countless examples have survived, and it is thanks to them that life can be breathed into the plans and reconstructions of the city that we owe to archaeological discovery.

The later legends

Babylon has also been a place of legend. Like no other city it was to be transformed and embellished in memory and culture, stimulating over two thousand years of reworking and re-imagining by artists and writers. For much of this time nothing was known of the city itself; so they turned to the Bible and especially to the accounts of ancient Greek historians, who took pains to find out about ancient Babylonia and record what they knew. Some of this information was very reliable; other elements look as if they were misunderstandings or even pure invention. Most commonly, later traditions blend Babylonian reality and reputation.

We owe to the Greeks the tradition of Seven Wonders of the World. The most familiar list today consists of the Great Pyramid of Giza, the Hanging Gardens of Babylon, the Statue of Zeus at Olympia, the Temple of Artemis

at Ephesus, the Mausoleum at Halicarnassus, the Colossus of Rhodes and the Lighthouse of Alexandria. Of these seven, six are well-attested archaeologically and their location known with certainty. One, the Great Pyramid at Giza in Egypt, even survives today. Only the Hanging Gardens of Babylon remain a mystery.

Ancient lists of the Wonders varied. According to some authorities Babylon could boast two: the Hanging Gardens and the city's enormous walls. Unlike the Gardens, the walls are altogether tangible, and have been identified and measured by archaeologists.

Babylon in the present

Modern archaeology and scholarship has brought much of ancient Babylon back to life for us, decoding texts on clay tablets and recovering ancient objects and structures. The most splendid of the monumental gateways that pierced Babylon's walls, the Ishtar Gate, has been excavated and painstakingly reconstructed in the Vorderasiatiches Museum in Berlin. Visitors who walk beneath its mighty arches today may glimpse for a moment the scale and power of the city of Nebuchadnezzar.

Guardians of the gate
The glazed brick surface of the Ishtar Gate complex was decorated with bulls and dragons.

Babylon in the imagination
When Lowell Thomas worked on his 1956 documentary
Cinerama film *Seven Wonders of the World*, the artist Mario
Larrinaga produced a set of atmospheric polychrome
paintings on glass. This one, *The Hanging Gardens of
Babylon*, is a copy commissioned shortly before the
destruction of the original.

KING NEBUCHADNEZZAR

King Nebuchadnezzar reigned for forty-three years, from 605 to 562 BC. He spent the treasury's silver on splendid buildings, and ruled Babylon in triumph during its period of greatest glory.

Yet later traditions have Nebuchadnezzar as a wicked ruler, who was struck down in his prime. The Bible relates that he was made mad and driven forth to live with wild beasts. Why has his reputation suffered so? It seems that the stories about Nebuchadnezzar's decline and fall may really relate to the later king Nabonidus (page 78). Nabonidus was an unpopular ruler, and it was during his reign that Babylon fell to the Persians. History has confused the two kings.

It was Nebuchadnezzar's father, Nabopolassar (626–605 BC), who set the stage for Babylon's extraordinary revival. Nabopolassar was a crucial player in the downfall of the Assyrian empire at Nineveh in 612 BC in partnership with the Medes of Western Iran. Crown Prince Nebuchadnezzar was a skilful military commander in his own right, and was on campaign in the West when his father died suddenly in 605 BC. Although his Neo-Babylonian dynasty was young, Nebuchadnezzar was able to return and claim the throne of what was now a real empire with no apparent opposition. After consolidating his holdings and dealing with threats from Egypt he was able to turn his attention to domestic affairs in Babylon. He was responsible for many great building projects that made his capital city renowned far and wide.

In 597 and again in 587 BC, Nebuchadnezzar laid siege to Jerusalem, the Judean capital. The deportation of the Judaeans to Babylon that followed was an event of momentous implications. The Babylonian Captivity is undoubtedly partly responsible for the negative image of Nebuchadnezzar that has come down to us.

The records that Nebuchadnezzar himself left for posterity tell a different story, of a great king confident in his righteousness and power.

For all the world to see

No-one could ever doubt the name of the king who
built Babylon. This huge panel from the Ishtar gate
complex shows Nebuchadnezzar's name and titles in
elegant cuneiform signs which have been moulded
and glazed in the very bricks.

'Brick for stone and tar for mortar'

Many of Babylon's building bricks were inscribed or stamped with the name and titles of Nebuchadnezzar in archaic writing. The message was designed for his peers, for future kings and for the gods.

On this particular brick one of the workmen, Zabina', has also written his own name in Aramaic letters before the clay hardened.

Nebuchadnezzar and Jerusalem
Nebuchadnezzar's first campaign against Jerusalem and
King Jehoiachin in 597 BC, described in the biblical
Books of Kings and Chronicles, was also recorded on
this cuneiform tablet by his own court chronicler:

*'He encamped against the city of Judah and on the second
day of the month Adar
he captured the city and seized its king'*

The mad king?

William Blake's hand-finished colour print *Nebuchadnezzar*, made around 1795–1805, depicts a king half-way between man and beast. In the Bible the mad Nebuchadnezzar is said to have spent seven years in the wilderness, living like an animal. The likelihood is that the story of the king in exile was really based upon the later ruler Nabonidus, who was vilified for his long absence from Babylon and for neglecting the state god, Marduk.

DRAGONS AND GODS

Babylon's patron deity, Marduk, had not always been the most important god in the ancient Mesopotamian pantheon. His rise to spiritual prominence was directly tied to Babylon's political fortunes, and, like other Mesopotamian gods, his identity was entwined with that of his city. He had both a home (the great temple Esagil) and a physical presence (his cult statue) in Babylon. The Babylonian Creation epic describes how he defeated the forces of Chaos and created the world. Despite Marduk's prominence, however, Babylon supported a huge cohort of deities, and the city was home to hundreds of temples and smaller shrines. Other major gods included Ishtar, Nabu, Adad and Sin, the Moon god.

Gods were embodied in their statues: when images were taken in procession as part of a religious rite the gods themselves travelled. Lengthy texts describe the New Year Festival at Babylon, during which Marduk travelled in state through the Ishtar Gate and out of the city to the appropriate temple.

The dragon, or *mushhushshu*, was particularly sacred to Marduk. It combined elements of serpent, lion and eagle. The Babylonian name, loaned from the much older Sumerian language, literally means 'angry snake'. Perhaps their nature reflects giant lizards that were kept somewhere in the temple.

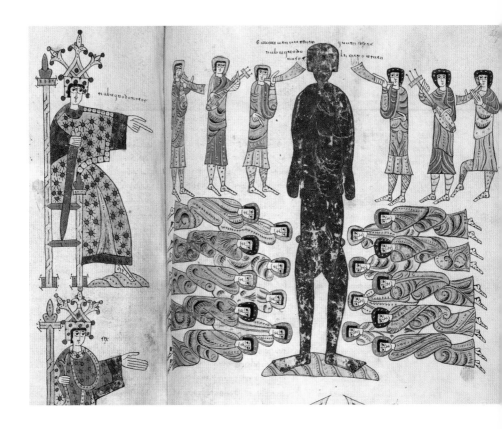

Idol worship

The Babylonians were condemned in the Bible for worshipping golden idols, probably statues of the Babylonian state god Marduk. Here the medieval *Silos Apocalypse* shows worshippers in front of such an idol. King Nebuchadnezzar is enthroned to the left.

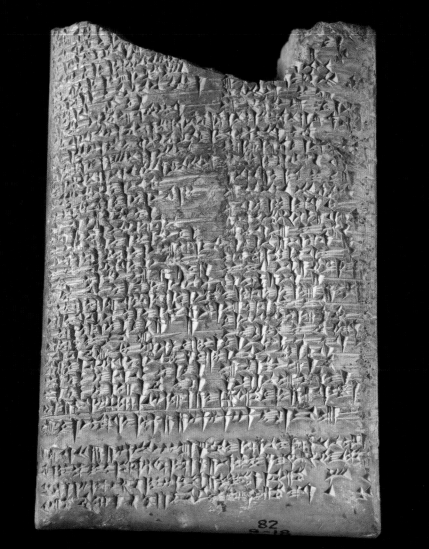

The creation of the world
One of the seven clay tablets that made up the Babylonian Creation epic, known as *Enuma Elish*. Those who heard this great poem recited out loud learned of the struggle against Chaos and the creation of mankind out of divine blood and clay to serve the gods for all time. The Epic championed the elevation of the god Marduk as head of the pantheon. This process involved the creation and centralization of Babylon as the centre of Mesopotamian culture.

FOLLOWING PAGES
Dragon, glazed brick panel
'… savage *mushhushshus*, who spatter enemy and foe with deadly venom'

A dragon in close-up

This *mushhushshu* is made of bronze, with a stump
of iron tongue still preserved. It was probably once
colourfully inlaid, and seems likely to have been on
guard in a prominent position.

Underground defences
This statue was discovered buried beneath a doorway
in the Southern Palace of Nebuchadnezzar. It would
have been placed there as protection against evil
spirits. The special headdress, with horns curving
around it, identifies the figure as a god.

Many gods or one?

For over two thousand years ancient Mesopotamians had acknowledged a vast pantheon. By the sixth century BC, however, the idea was emerging that there might be one central and all-encompassing deity of whom the other important gods were merely aspects. The idea is applied in this tablet to Marduk; later a similar view was held by some of the Moon god, Sin. It is likely that such texts were theological speculation that never directly affected the population at large.

'*Ninurta* is Marduk of the hoe
Nergal is Marduk of war
Zababa is Marduk of battle
Enlil is Marduk of lordship and deliberation
Nabu is Marduk of accounting
Sin is Marduk as illuminator of the night
Shamash is Marduk of justice'

THE TEMPLE TOWER OF BABYLON

At the centre of the city stood the ziggurat, the temple tower. It was named Etemenanki, the Foundation Platform of Heaven and Earth. Connected to the most important temple, Esagil, it acted as both a physical and a spiritual link between Babylon, the centre of the human world and the residence of Marduk himself, and heaven directly above. It communicated, therefore, a mixture of symbolic values to all who lived by it, or ever encountered it. Its size is known to have been 91 square metres at the base, with a height probably well over 70 metres. The top level housed a temple, but we are still not sure about the rites or rituals that took place in it.

In later centuries the temple tower vanished almost completely. Nebuchadnezzar's bricks were of such high quality that the building, once ruined, came eventually to be treated as a giant quarry. Etemenanki achieved a different permanence long after the building itself disappeared. It was the model for the Tower of Babel in the Bible, where it became the undying symbol of human arrogance and overreaching folly.

It was the Tower above all that captivated artists. From the Middle Ages to our own time, this image has been a lasting inspiration.

Esagil Tablet

Long after the time of Nebuchadnezzar a teacher of mathematics produced this classroom treatise on measuring great buildings, focusing on the huge Esagil Temple. Its detailed information has been of direct use to archaeologists concerned with reconstructing the building itself.

A Tower to reach Heaven
The Tower of Babel as imagined by
Lucas van Valckenborch in 1595.
The fantastic building, so tall that
its summit reaches into the clouds,
swarms with hundreds of human
figures. Parts of the building appear
to be hewn from a gigantic natural
rock.

Nebuchadnezzar's ziggurat in reconstruction
There have been endless theories and successive
models, but this new reconstruction of the ziggurat
is based on what we now know from excavations and
ancient texts. The details of the temple on the top
level remain uncertain.

The human figures in the model give some idea of the
scale of the building, and help us imagine what it must
have been like to climb the colossal main staircase.

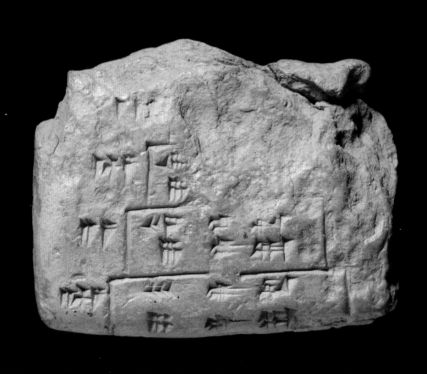

A pupil's exercise
This school drawing shows a ziggurat in elevation.
Its base is given as only 21 metres per side, so if the
students were examining the ziggurat of Babylon it
must have been an exercise in planning to scale.

FOLLOWING PAGES

A king before a tower
Hard stone cylinder seals, used instead of a signature,
were usually carved with scenes cut in reverse. Here a
king performs a religious ritual in front of a five-storey
ziggurat. What the fox and the fish are doing is not
clear. This seal was already a thousand years old when
was buried in a grave in the centre of Babylon at the
time of Nebuchadnezzar's dynasty.

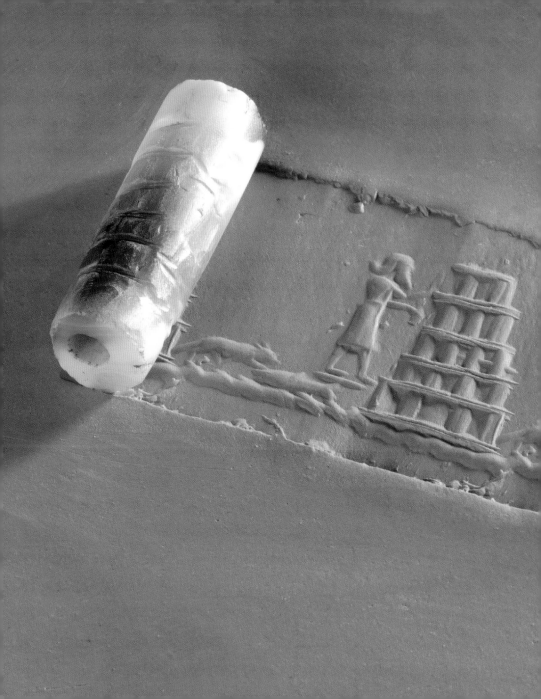

The Tower topples

Later artists could only imagine the
Tower of Babel, and depicted the
building and its fate in many forms.
Cornelis Anthonisz produced this
engraving in 1547, and was the first
to use the Roman Colosseum as a
model for the Tower.

The ghost of the ziggurat
All that remained of Babylon's greatest monument
in 1973: rectangular ditches filled with murky water.
The projection to the south was the main staircase.

ROYAL GARDENS

We do not know where at the site the Hanging Gardens of Babylon were, or indeed, whether they ever really existed. We do know that ancient Mesopotamian kings valued their gardens, and some used them for exotic plants and animals. If Nebuchadnezzar, as the stories say, really built a wonderful garden paradise for Amyitis, his homesick queen, archaeology has so far failed to locate it.

According to the Sicilian author Diodorus, writing in the first century BC:

When the ascending terraces had been built, there had been constructed beneath them galleries which carried the entire weight of the planted garden and rose little by little one above the other along the approach…

Babylon in bloom

This artist's impression, first published in 1927, incorporates the results of Robert Koldewey's excavations at Babylon to give an idea of the city at its height. Koldewey once thought he had found a location for the Hanging Gardens, and this picture incorporates his ideas.

A royal kitchen garden

Mesopotamian kings were proud of their gardens.
On this clay tablet are listed the entire contents of
the garden of the eighth-century BC Babylonian king
Marduk-apla-iddina (biblical Merodach-Baladan).
The first column includes onions, shallots and garlic,
no doubt destined for the king's favourite soups.

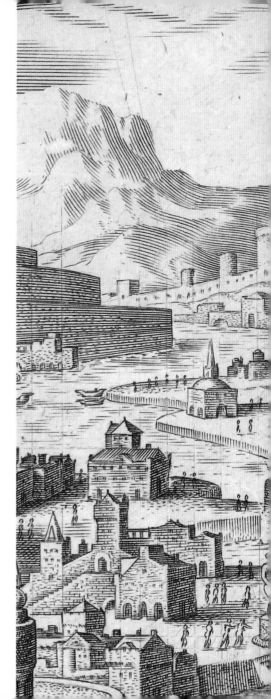

Picturing the Gardens
This palatial structure, Maarten van Heemskerck's 16th-century interpretation of classical descriptions of the Hanging Gardens, would have been more at home in the landscape of his own day.

STATELY BEASTS

Nebuchadnezzar was a hugely wealthy king, so he was never inhibited in demanding the best from his architects. Babylon's palaces were sumptuous. As well as two enormous residences in the centre of the city, Nebuchadnezzar and his court could take refuge in a large and well-ventilated 'Summer Palace' to the north, escaping the worst of the heat and smells of the metropolis.

The most famous of his achievements are the Processional Way and the Ishtar Gate. These were excavated at the beginning of the 20th century by Robert Koldewey and reconstructed to spectacular effect in the Vorderasiatisches Museum in Berlin. The Ishtar Gate was Babylon's grandest entrance. Clad entirely in deep blue glazed bricks and bedecked with relief images of hundreds of marching bulls and dragons, the sight greeting an ancient visitor to the capital must have been unforgettable. Through the Ishtar Gate ran the broad Processional Way, lined on both sides by reliefs of striding lions. At certain points in the year state ritual required processions of the gods and other displays for which the excited populace must have lined the walls in huge numbers.

Lion, glazed brick panel

Bull, glazed brick panel
Alongside the dragons of the Ishtar Gate stood bulls.
Bulls were particularly linked with Adad, the storm god.

PREVIOUS PAGES
Lion, glazed brick panel
Nebuchadnezzar's pacing lions seem sedate, but power
and energy are carefully reflected in the moulding, and
their stark symbolism is unmistakable.

WRITING AND IDEAS

Writing in Babylon was already very ancient by the time of Nebuchadnezzar. Experiments in recording speech through signs impressed into clay with a reed took place well before 3000 BC. Much later the king's learned men not only had extensive libraries of clay tablets, but also investigated the origin of their own script, collecting extremely ancient texts and analysing their signs. Few individuals were truly literate in Nebuchadnezzar's time, since the cuneiform (meaning 'wedge-shaped') script used to write the Babylonian language contained hundreds of characters and took years to master.

From these tablets we can discover the daily life, political events, religious beliefs and literary accomplishments of Babylon in its heyday. Clay, even when unbaked, survives in the ground in a way that was altogether unanticipated by ancient scribes. This means that purely ephemeral documents come to us in profusion, as well as official records and those deliberately buried as a message for the future.

Around this time, Aramaic came to supplant Babylonian as the everyday language, so the Aramaic alphabetic script, written on leather and skin, eventually displaced cuneiform writing altogether.

The Babylonian Mappa Mundi (see page 67)

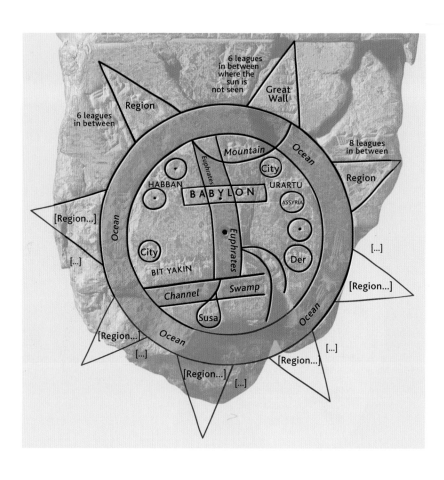

6 leagues
in between
where the
sun is
not seen

Great
Wall

Region

6 leagues
in between

8 leagues
in between

Region

Mountain

Ocean

Euphrates

City

HABBAN

B A B Y L O N

URARTU

ASSYRIA

[Region...]

Ocean

Euphrates

[...]

City

[...]

Der

BIT YAKIN

[Region...]

Channel

Swamp

Ocean

[Region...]

Susa

[...]

Ocean

[...]

[Region...]

[Region...]

[...]

OPPOSITE AND PREVIOUS PAGE

Mappa Mundi

Babylon was the centre of the universe, and this, the oldest world map, proves it. Regions both real and mythological are shown from a bird's eye view, with the human world ringed by a bitter sea with remote islands. Nebuchadnezzar's capital city straddles the Euphrates River, by far the largest of the habitations which are shown.

A record of Nebuchadnezzar's successes

Monumental, elegant and calligraphically superb, this beautiful stone inscription records the great achievements of Nebuchadnezzar's reign. The old-fashioned cuneiform signs must have been drawn out for the mason by one of the best scribes in the kingdom. The object itself intentionally resembles a giant clay tablet.

This is widely known today as the 'East India House Inscription' because it was presented to the East India House Museum by Sir Harford Jones Bridges, from where it came to the British Museum in 1938.

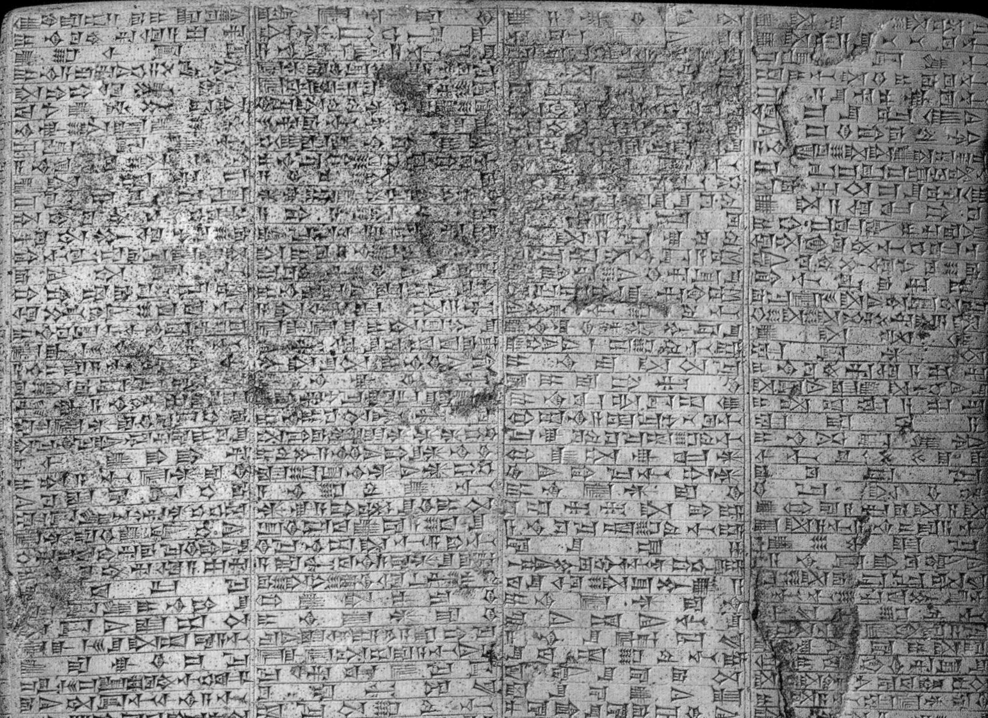

Writing from the beginning of time
A fragment from an esoteric Babylonian writing manual. The ancient 'picture' forms of the cuneiform signs are drawn, together with a secret number for each sign. Armed with this a scribe could imitate the oldest writing in the world, or produce limited-access documents in impenetrable number code.

An original Babel-fish?

The right flank of this bronze dogfish shows two fins, but the left side only one. To the Babylonians this abnormality in a real fish carried serious implications, and a permanent record was required. In this case the fish was modelled in clay, the omen written out along its sides, and a cast produced in bronze. The omen reads:

'If a fish lacks a left fin (?), a foreign army will be destroyed.
The 12th year of Nebuchadnezzar, king of Babylon,
son of Nabopolassar, king of Babylon.'

No specific military triumph can yet be linked with this date, 592 BC, but the rarity of the object suggests that a major event lay behind it.

Babylon was a centre for learning of all kinds, especially divination – the use of omens to predict the future. Once reserved for the king and state, fortune-telling came to be relied on by many private individuals in later periods. Many kinds of divination existed, but one of the most important was observation of the heavens. Celestial observations were recorded over many centuries, making it possible to predict certain astral events. In addition, the importance of the stars as providing omens in themselves led to the development of astrology and the zodiac.

Babylonian knowledge also had its influence on Hippocratic medicine. The two systems shared a reliance on observation and the careful cataloguing of symptoms and treatments as well as training by apprenticeship. As with astronomy and mathematics, Babylonian experts left us no theoretical writings, and assessment of their exact medical knowledge is still a matter for investigation.

One indirect legacy of Babylonian scholarship is our division of the day into twenty-four hours, with hours and minutes divided into sixtieths. The Babylonians used sexagesimal numbers (base 60 instead of base 10) for their calculations because the number 60 can be neatly divided by so many different whole numbers. This system was adopted by Greek scholars and eventually applied to measuring time.

The zodiac in transmission

Astrology and the signs of the zodiac were Babylonian inventions. Elements of this system survived the extinction of cuneiform script in the early centuries AD because it was copied appreciatively from Babylonian into Greek, and on into later astrology. This 1840 Sanskrit treatise compares European, Islamic and Hindu zodiacs, all of which are descended from the Babylonian system.

FOLLOWING PAGES

How to make a water clock

This remarkable composition – known as MUL.APIN, 'The Plough Constellation' – includes lists of the stars and constellations, schemes for predicting risings and settings of the planets and even explains how to measure the lengths of daylight with a water clock or sun-shadows. It was compiled by many scholars between 1000 and 700 BC. The water-clock had to be adjusted to accommodate the longer hours of days in summer.

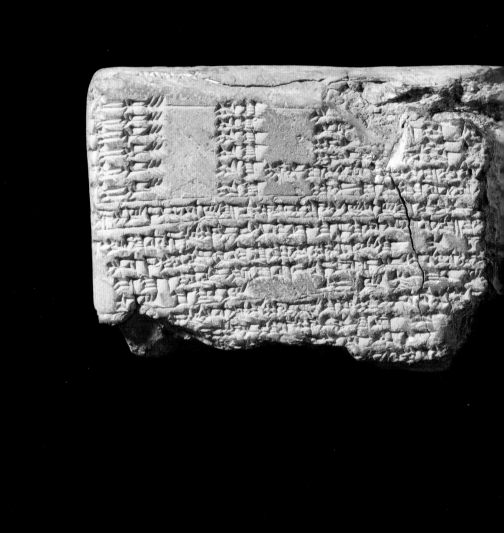

KING NABONIDUS

Nabonidus (556–539 BC) was a very unusual king, breaking with traditional religious practice and even abandoning Babylon itself. A devout follower of the Moon god Sin, he quit his homeland and travelled to distant Teima in Arabia. His son Belshazzar, meanwhile, acted as regent in the capital during his father's ten-year absence. By the time Nabonidus returned, Babylon was threatened by a new power in the east. In 539 BC the victorious Persian army under Cyrus II entered the city without resistance, and brought to an end the Neo-Babylonian dynasty.

According to sources hostile to Nabonidus, one of the king's worst sins in leaving Babylon was that his absence prevented the important New Year Festival from taking place. The festival lasted from the 1st to the 12th of *Nisannu* (April), and culminated in the king's 'taking the hand of Bel,' a ritual tradition that was essential to guarantee the well-being of the state for the coming year. Bel is another name for the god Marduk.

Nabonidus

King Nabonidus stands beneath symbols of his gods, most prominently the Moon. The royal inscription that once filled much of the empty space was erased on the orders of Cyrus after the Persian takeover.

The king and the Moon god
A royal message for the future,
an inscribed cylinder of clay buried
as a time-capsule. Nabonidus has
rebuilt the ziggurat of the Moon
god Sin at the city of Ur, and prays
that he and his son, Belshazzar, be
safeguarded from wrong-doing.

BABYLON AND AFTER

The familiar image of an apocalyptic Fall of Babylon is misleading. When Cyrus II captured the city from Nabonidus and made it part of the Achaemenid Persian Empire in 539 BC, it continued uninterruptedly as a very important capital. Babylon's political significance was undiminished by the time of Alexander the Great. Alexander intended it to function as the capital of his world empire but died in the city in 323 BC. After this the empire fractured and fragmented, with Seleucus I, one of Alexander's generals, gaining dominance in Western Asia. Babylon was gradually superseded by the newly-founded Seleucia-on-the-Tigris, which enticed merchants and trade away from the venerable capital. In the end Babylon was to fade rather than fall, and more through economic factors than military might.

By the time Baghdad was founded in AD 764, Babylon had sunk into obscurity, and by the tenth century AD only a village remained. By the twelfth century even this had vanished. Babylon, once the greatest city in the world, remained visible only as a muddle of nondescript mounds on the Mesopotamian plain. It was to be some seven hundred years before archaeologists began to rediscover the wonders of Nebuchadnezzar's city.

The Aramaic alphabet in cuneiform

A school exercise tablet which dates from about 500 BC, by which time Aramaic was the lingua franca of Babylon. On this unique tablet the sounds of the Aramaic alphabet letters, such as would be learned by a child, are written in the ancient cuneiform script. This document must have been written by a pupil who was bilingual in Babylonian and Aramaic.

The Aramaic letter-sounds given in the tablet are printed in the box, left. The letter order has survived and is similar to our modern alphabet.

a	la
be	me
ge	nu
da	sa
e	a-a-nu
u	pe
za	tsu
he	qu
te	re
ia	shi
ka	ta

The Writing on the Wall

Belshazzar's Feast, depicted by Rembrandt in about 1636. The Writing on the Wall prophesied the downfall of Belshazzar's Babylon. In the Bible only Daniel is able to read the Aramaic inscription. Here the Hebrew characters in which it is written are arranged in vertical columns (instead of the usual right to left). This provides a plausible explanation of why the king was unable to read the writing, even though Aramaic was the everyday language of his court.

In reality Belshazzar was the crown prince (son of Nabonidus) and never the king of Babylon.

The Cyrus Cylinder

This is one of the most famous cuneiform inscriptions ever discovered. It was buried in the foundations of the city wall of Babylon after the capture of the city by the Persian king Cyrus II in 539 BC. Cyrus, here portrayed as the tool and servant of the god Marduk, is to rectify the chaos caused in Babylon by Nabonidus and is welcomed by the population.

The Cyrus Cylinder is sometimes referred to as a 'Charter of Human Rights'. Such a concept would have been quite alien to Cyrus's world, and the written text of the cylinder, a skilful political document with quite different preoccupations, says nothing of human rights.

Alexander at the gates of Babylon

This Babylonian Chronicle documents the arrival of
Alexander the Great at the gates of Babylon in 330 BC.
Local priests warned him that were he to enter, he was
doomed to die within the city's walls. Alexander is
recorded as entering undeterred, declaring: 'I will not
go into your houses,' and undertaking to rebuild the
Esagil temple.

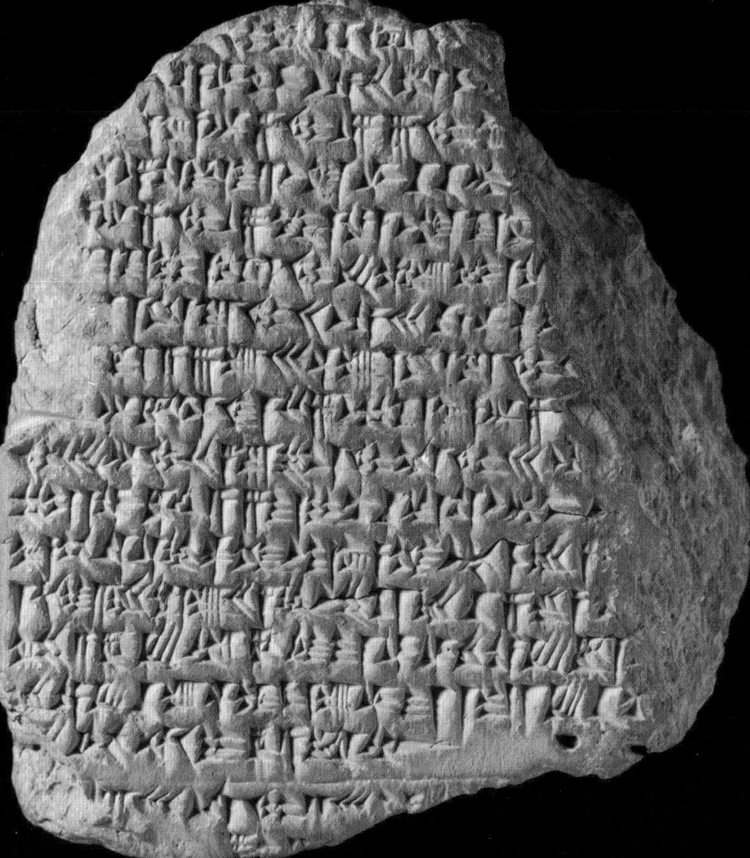

Greek and Babylonian in the classroom
For Greeks at the end of the first millennium BC, access
to Babylonian scientific information meant having to
learn cuneiform script. Their school exercises show a
Greek pronunciation 'crib' on one side of the clay tablet
to help with the Babylonian cuneiform on the other.
This example in Greek writing gives individual Sumerian
signs, their pronunciation and their 'sign names' as
found in a traditional curricular list.

Beyond Babylon

In the New Testament Book of Revelation the name
Babylon is used as a cipher for Rome, and the invective
directed against the city in the Old Testament is also
transferred. The image of the Whore of Babylon,
depicted by Albrecht Dürer in this woodcut of about
1496, shows how the real city of Babylon and its mythic
image as a City of Sin grew apart over the centuries.

ILLUSTRATION ACKNOWLEDGEMENTS

Frontispiece: Glazed brick panel from the throne room of Nebuchadnezzar, Staatliche Museen zu Berlin, Vorderasiatisches Museum. © bpk/SMB Vorderasiatisches Museum, Berlin/Klaus Göken.

Pp 8–9 and 12: Reconstruction of the Ishtar Gate at the Staatliche Museen zu Berlin, Vorderasiatisches Museum. © bpk/SMB Vorderasiatisches Museum, Berlin/Olaf M. Tessmer.

p. 15: Mario Larrinaga, *The Hanging Gardens of Babylon*, AD 1959–62, oil on canvas. © Ancient Wonders, Inc., Brighton, Michigan USA.

p.18: Detail of a glazed brick relief with inscription of Nebuchadnezzar from the Ishtar Gate reconstruction in the Staatliche Museen zu Berlin, Vorderasiatisches Museum. © bpk/SMB Vorderasiatisches Museum, Berlin/Olaf M. Tessmer.

p. 21: Inscribed brick of Nebuchadnezzar. British Museum, BM 90136. Photo © The Trustees of the British Museum.

p. 22: Chronicle of Nebuchadnezzar. British Museum, 21946. Photo © The Trustees of the British Museum.

p. 24-5. William Blake, *Nebuchadnezzar*, AD 1795/c.1805, colour print finished in ink and watercolour on paper. Tate Britain N05059. © Tate, London.

p. 27: Detail of manuscript illumination from the *Silos Apocalypse*, London, British Library Add. MS 11695, detail of ff. 228v–229. © The British Library Board.

p. 28: The Babylonian Creation Epic. British Museum, BM 93016. Photo © The Trustees of the British Museum.

Pp 30-1: Glazed brick panel of a dragon. Staatliche Museen zu Berlin, Vorderasiatisches Museum, VA Bab 4431. © Olaf M. Tessmer/ SMB-Vorderasiatisches Museum Berlin.

p. 32: Bronze head of a dragon. Musée du Louvre, AO 4106. Photo RMN/© Franck Raux.

p. 35: Statue of a god. Staatliche Museen zu Berlin, Vorderasiatisches Museum, VA Bab 3135. © Olaf M. Tessmer/ SMB-Vorderasiatisches Museum Berlin.

p. 36: Monotheism tablet. British Museum, BM 47406. Photo © The Trustees of the British Museum.

p. 39: Esagil tablet. Musée du Louvre, AO 6555. Photo RMN/Christian Jean/Jean Schormans.

Pp 40-1: Lucas van Valckenborch, *The Tower of Babel*, AD 1595, oil on panel. Mittelrhein-Museum Koblenz, MRM M 31.

p. 43: Scale model of the ziggurat Etemenanki. Staatliche Museen zu Berlin, Vorderasiatisches Museum, VAG 1284. © Olaf M. Tessmer/ SMB-Vorderasiatisches Museum Berlin.

p. 44: A school tablet with a drawing of a ziggurat in elevation. British Museum, BM 38217. Photo © The Trustees of the British Museum.

Pp 46-7: Cylinder seal depicting a ziggurat with modern impression. Staatliche Museen zu Berlin, Vorderasiatisches Museum, VA 7736. © Olaf M. Tessmer/ SMB-Vorderasiatisches Museum Berlin.

48-9: Cornelis Anthonisz Teunissen, *Fall of the Tower of Babel*, AD 1547, engraving. British Museum, PD 1871,1209.4631. Photo © The Trustees of the British Museum.

p. 50: Aerial photograph of Babylon showing the remains of the ziggurat. © Georg Gerster/Panos.

p. 53: Herbert Anger, *View of the Ishtar Gate and Processional Way*, colour print after watercolour, 1927. © bpk/SBB/Ruth Schacht.

p. 54: Clay tablet with a list of plants in the garden of Marduk-apla-iddina. British Museum, BM 46226. Photo © The Trustees of the British Museum.

Pp 56-7: Philips Galle after Maarten van Heemskerck, *The Walls of Babylon*, AD 1572, engraving (detail). British Museum, PD 1875,0508.46. Photo © The Trustees of the British Museum.

p. 59: Glazed brick panel showing a lion. Staatliche Museen zu Berlin, Vorderasiatisches Museum, © bpk/SMB Vorderasiatisches Museum, Berlin/Olaf M. Tessmer.

Pp 60-1: Glazed brick panel showing a lion. Musée du Louvre, AO 21118. Photo © RMN/Franck Raux.

p. 63: Glazed brick panel showing a bull from the Ishtar Gate. Staatliche Museen zu Berlin, Vorderasiatisches Museum, VA Bab 4431. © bpk/SMB Vorderasiatisches Museum, Berlin/Olaf M. Tessmer.

p. 65: The Babylonian Map of the World tablet. British Museum, BM 92687. Photo © The Trustees of the British Museum.

p. 66: Diagram of the Map of the World tablet by Paul Goodhead.

p. 69: The East India House inscription. British Museum, BM 129397. Photo © The Trustees of the British Museum.

p. 70: Fragment from a Babylonian writing manual. British Museum, BM 93016. Photo © The Trustees of the British Museum.

p. 72: Oracular fish. Staatliche Museen zu Berlin, Vorderasiatisches Museum, VA Bab 4374. © Olaf M. Tessmer/ SMB-Vorderasiatisches Museum Berlin.

Pp 74-5: MUL.APIN ('The Plough Constellation') tablet. British Museum BM 42277. Photo © The Trustees of the British Museum.

p. 77: Page from a Sanskrit treatise on the zodiac, *Durgāshankara Pāthaka, Sarvasiddhārtatattvacūdamani (Crest-Jewel of the Essence of all Systems of Astronomy)*, AD 1840. British Library MS Or 5259, ff. 56v-5. © The British Library Board.

p. 79: Stela of Nabonidus. British Museum BM 90837. Photo © The Trustees of the British Museum.

p. 80: Barrel cylinder of Nabonidus with foundation inscription. British Museum BM 91125. Photo © The Trustees of the British Museum.

p. 83: School tablet with Aramaic alphabet in cuneiform. British Museum BM 25636. Photo © The Trustees of the British Museum.

Pp 84-5: Rembrandt Harmenszoon van Rijn, *Belshazzar's Feast*, c.1636, oil on canvas. National Gallery, NG6350. © National Gallery, London, UK/The Bridgeman Art Library.

Pp 86-7: The Cyrus Cylinder. British Museum, BM 90920. Photo © The Trustees of the British Museum.

p. 89: Babylonian Chronicle with account of Alexander arriving at the gates of Babylon. British Museum BM 36761. Photo © The Trustees of the British Museum.

p. 90: Fragment of school tablet with Greek writing. British Museum BM 35458. Photo © The Trustees of the British Museum.

p. 93: Albrecht Dürer, *The Whore of Babylon, The Destruction of Babylon, and the Knight Called Faithful and True*, c. AD 1496–7, woodcut. British Museum PD E. 4.4143. Photo © The Trustees of the British Museum.